Are You Ready?

by

W.B. Godbey

First Fruits Press
Wilmore,
Kentucky
c2018

Are you ready?
By W.B. Godbey.
First Fruits Press, © 2018

ISBN: 9781621718246 (print), 9781621718253 (digital), 9781621718260
(kindle)

Digital version at https://place.asburyseminary.edu/godbey/19/

For all other uses, contact:

First Fruits Press
B.L. Fisher Library
Asbury Theological Seminary
204 N. Lexington Ave.
Wilmore, KY 40390
http://place.asburyseminary.edu/firstfruits

Godbey, W. B. (William Baxter), 1833-1920.
   Are you ready? / by W.B. Godbey. – Wilmore, KY : First Fruits Press,
   ©2018.

   pages ; cm.

   Reprint. Previously published: Greensboro, N.C. : Apostolic Messenger
   Office, [190-?]
   ISBN: 9781621718246 (pbk.)

   1. Redemption--Christianity. 2. Salvation--Christianity. I. Title.

BT775.G622 2018

Cover design by Jon Ramsay

asburyseminary.edu
800.2ASBURY
204 North Lexington Avenue
Wilmore, Kentucky 40390

First Fruits
THE ACADEMIC OPEN PRESS OF ASBURY SEMINARY

First Fruits Press
The Academic Open Press of Asbury Theological Seminary
204 N. Lexington Ave., Wilmore, KY 40390
859-858-2236
first.fruits@asburyseminary.edu
asbury.to/firstfruits

Are You Ready?

By

W. B. Godbey

AUTHOR OF
"New Testament Commentaries." "New Testament
Translation," and a great number of
other books and booklets.

PUBLISHED BY

THE APOSTOLIC MESSENGER OFFICE

GREENSBORO, N. C.

Are You Ready?

The great reason why it is so imperatively encumbant on us all to get ready to meet God is the simple fact that no human being is ready without His personal redeeming grace, which normally reaches all far back in the prenatal state, the moment soul and body united constitute personality, which is five or six months antecedently to the physical birth Heb. 2: 9, "By the grace of God, Christ tasted death for everyone not as e.v. "every man", as the Greek **buper pantos** literally means everyone, i.e. every human being. Therefore the very moment soul and body unite constitute personality, the omnipotent redeeming grace of God in Christ comes into availability, superinducing a free and full justification on heaven's chancery in the normal gracious economy invariably followed by the resurrection of the dead soul wrought by the Holy Ghost in the heart; superinducing the gloriously consolitory fact that by the omnipotent grace of God in Christ through His vicarious substitutionary atonement every human being is actually born a Christian as that cognomen, the **sunum desideradum,** chief desire of every human being, simply means a soul saved by Christ. What a triumphant victory, our wonderful Savior thus achieves on Satan in the transcendant reality that He actually lassoes every soul far back in the prenatal state before it is born into the world; utterly regardless of environments, in the palace or the hovel; the camp meeting or the brothel; the Bible College or the saloon; every human being is born a Christian, as we see abundantly confirmed by our Savior's treatment of the babies, everywhere taking them in His arms and certifying, "of such is my kingdom"; thus authenticating their claim to citizenship and their right to membership in the visible church, signified by symbolic baptism, and with due attention on the part of parents, guardians and pastors, would all in the succession of the prophet Samuel, John the Baptist, the Apostle Timothy, your humble servant and a mighty host of others be happily converted antecedently to the forfeiture of their infantile justification followed in due time by the great second work of grace, entire sanctification, giving them a clean heart thus leading them out of spiritual infancy into adult age, developing championship in the kingdom and a place in the bridehood, catalogued with the prolonged faithroll Heb 11 ch.

(d) Why need they conversion if they are already Christians? From the simple fact that while justified freely in heaven for Christ's sake alone the moment soul and body united constitute personality and regenerated by the Holy Spirit responsively to that justification, which he cannot do till the law is satisfied, whereas in that case He is never delinquent in the felicitious execution of His mighty work, i.e. the new creation; thus destroying the works of Satan 1 John 3:8 and restoring all things, even in the grand ultimatum, back to the Edenic state Acts 3: 19-25, the infant while thus freely justified in heaven and regenerated by the Holy Spirit is full of hereditary depravity transmitted from Satan through Adam the first our federal head, which turns his face away from God toward this wicked world, sin, Satan and hell; so that it not turned round, which is the literal meaning of conversion and introduced to the Savior like the prodigal son He will spontaneously go into sin as soon as he reaches responsibility; thus forfeiting his justification and becoming a backslider as you see abundantly demonstrated in the case of the prodigal son who had wandered far from his father's house and wasted his patrimony in rictous living but melting the good fortune to get rescued from the hog pen rested out of Satan's clutches and make his escape all the way back to his father's home; thus showing up most incontestably a glorious reclamation, popularly denominated a briliant conversion.

(e) You see clearly from this case which parallels every sinner, converted to God, is simply a reclamation; whereas the elder brother having felicitously been converted in his infancy, i.e. turned around and introduced to His Father so receiving the sweet inundations of his paternal affection and redeeming grace, he became so interested as to never wander away and waste his patrimony like his younger brother. Oh the profound sleep wrapping pulpit and pew in lethean slumber appertaining to the infantile membership of God's church! We rejoice now in the glorious dawn of the millennium brilliantly adonbrated withersoever we turn our enchanted vision; saluted by the roar of machinery doing the work of the world, the scream of the locomotive, the bugle of the electric train and the precipitate sweep of the automobiles, all proclaiming the near proximity of the glorious King riding down on His millenial throne, to dethrone Satan and envelop the globe with the splendor of His glory, till he shall have dominion over river, sea and shore, far as the eagle's pinion or the dove's light wing can soar, all roaring out the jubilant proclamation, "of all the mighty nations in the east or in the west, or this glorious Yankee nation, is the greatest and the best! From the great Atlantic Ocean, where the day begins to dawn, leap across the rocking mountains far away to Oregon! Oh these great and mighty rivers, that course along our hills, are just the thing for washing sheep, and driving cotton mills! Our mountains, lakes and rivers, are all a blaze of fire, and we send the news by lightning on the telegraphic wire! The hero chieftan laying

down his pen closes his eyes in Washington at ten.
the lightning currier leaps along the line and tells
the St. Louis tale at nine; haulting a 1000 miles,
whence he departed, and getting there an 'hour
before he started! When the millenium reaches us
in its heavenly inundations, the normal order of do-
mestic life will be the happy conversion of all the
children before they lose their infantile justification followed speedily by the crowning victory of
entire sanctification, thus legitimately superinduced
by Satan's dethronement and ejectment into hell,
to howl a prisoner a thousand years, amid the lugi-
brious wails of his myrmydons having been ske-
daddled from the globe, precipitatedly retreating
before the inundating billows of heavenly glory, des-
tined to cover the earth, as the waters the sea.

CHAPTER I

WHY MUST I GET READY?

From the simple and indisputable fact that no human being is ready, until omnipotent grace pre-
pares them to meet their God, Amos 4:12. When
God created Adam He created the race, as he was
the seed of humanity and you read Gen. 1 ch. "Everything had its seed within its self; Eve no exception to the unity of humanity in Adam as she was
not a **de moro** creation, but metamorphism of
Adam's rib, and consequently created with Adam;
this transformation really making her the second
blessing in creation; her moral and spiritual superiority in all ages and nations, abundantly demonstrated thus showing up the fact that she is better
by nature and by grace than the rougher and hard-
er sex; more easily saved; more Christian women
on the earth than men, and of course more in heav-
en, the masculine wing of humanity having the majority in earth and hell,—an indisputable fact which

puts a signal rebuke on the popular mistake of shouting over the boys and weeping over the girls born in the homes of every nation. whereas pertinancy would superinduce the reverse; normally concluded from the ostensible fact that life is a failure if we do not get saved; as in case of poor Judas, the fallen apostle, of whom Jesus said, "better for that man that he had never been born" as you see Acts 1 ch, dying of suicide "he went to his own place, i.e. hell, i.e. God's penitentiary, for the incarceration of all the people who will not let Him save them as 'tis absolutely certain that He does save every one who will let Him Ezek. 33:11; superinducing the irresistable conclusion that no soul makes his bed in hell fire unless under Satanic infatuation, taking the bit in his teeth and running away with the salvation wagon, precipitates it over the falls of damnation in irretrievable ruin engulfed in the unquenchable billows of a bottomless hell.

(f) Thus God makes every man bear his own responsibility, from the simple and undeniable fact, that He verily does save every one who will let Him. As He is omnipotent, why can He not save every one? Because He cannot contradict Himself. He has made us free moral agents to choose for ourselves, loyalty to Him which is life or the negative which is disharmony, separation, disloyalty, which simply means death, temporal, spiritual and eternal, as He alone is life and alienation from Him, death inevitable N. B. Death simply means separation when the branch is severed from the tree it is dead. When the soul is separated from the body it is dead and separated from God is spiritually dead through all eternity. When Satan fought the battle of Eden, he achieved the greatest victory of the ages as the whole human race had been seminally created in Adam. Therefore as God had said, "in the day that thou eateth thereof thou shalt

surely die." The moment he disobeyed God, he lost
his spiritual life, because God alone is life and everything severed from Him is dead. He did not say,
your mind shalt die, nor your body, "but thou shalt
surely die." Adam was an immortal spirit, in the
image and likeness of God, which is righteousness
and true holiness, Eph. 6:24. The mind is man's
grand induement in its transcendant superiority,
differentiating him from the animal creation, while
the body is simply the tenement in which he lives,
during mortality and probation, the mansion in
which the **psychee**, soul lives; but in the transfigured state, the house in which the **pneuma** spirit,
will abide for ever, similitudinous to the glorified
body of our Savior, manifested to Peter, James and
John on the Mt. of Transfiguration, Moses having
been resurrected for that occasion, Jude 9, appear-
ing there with Him in His transfigured body representing all the saints who will be transfigured by
the resurrection, including the sepulchered when
the Lord comes for His bride 1 Thess. 6 ch., and
Elijah also on that occasion, representing all who
will be transfigured by translation as he and Enoch
and all the saints who will be living on the earth
when the Lord comes for His bride; 1 Cor. 15:51
"We shall not all sleep but we shall all be changed,
in a moment, in a twinkling of an eye, for the
trumpet shall sound and we shall be changed," this
mortal shall put on immortality and death shall
be swallowed up in life.

(g) Christ was made manifest, that He might
destroy the works of the devil, 1 John 3:8 when He
preached to the Samaritan woman at Jacob's well,
she said to Him "we know that Messiah cometh who
will restore all things." He confessed that it was
true, at the same time responding to her, "I am He,"
excepting the truth which had floated on the atmos-
phere to the eyes of that heathen woman. In sancti-

fication, we receive spiritual restitution, whereas in glorification when the mortal shall put on immortality, we receive mental restoration, while the resurrection will destroy these bodies, from the mortality superinduced by the fall; the earth which God created for man and donated to him, with all the animals on the continents and islands and the fishes of the sea, and the birds that fly through the air. Pursuant to the great work for which Christ came into the world, not only will man be restored in his three natures spirit, mind and body; but this earth is to be restored back to him and to become his inheritance forever, so in the glorious coming ages after the final restitution, we can all invite the angels home with us, the saints will possess the restored and glorified earth forever.

(h) 1 Cor. 15:22 "In Adam all die, but in Christ shall all be made alive. Satan knew that Adam was the citadel of humanity, and consequently from the beginning made for him with all his might, utilizing the serpent and Eve as passports, transmitting him in his enterprise to capture Adam, thus achieving a victory whose magnitude, mortal tongue can never tell; because all the countless millions of oncoming generations, through rolling centuries, ages, and cycles wherein Adam and captured by the fatal satanic lasso of sin actual, imbred and hereditary; the loathsome leprosy utter incurable by all human device and thus not only enslaving Adam and Eve, but taking everything they had, dethroning both the king and queen and sitting down on the throne of the world, actually manipulating it as a hell feeder, to fatten souls for the barbucues of damnation. As man was created with the power of infinitesimal self repetition, when he lost his spiritual life, has still retained that power and has consequently filled the earth with spiritually dead people fit only for hell. When the news of the fall

reached heaven, the angels who had always taken
such an interest in this world, shouting jubilantly
when they saw it roll out from shapely chaos, responsively to the divine mandate and take its place
among concomitant world moving through their
orbits around the effulgent throne, with vociferous
shouts they answered the anthem of the morning
stars, i.e. the superior angels who sang together at
creation's birth.   Therefore when the sad news of
the fall reached them, they would all with enthu-
siasm have joined in a campaign for the rescue; but
fully   assured of   their utter   incompetency they
hung their harps upon the willows and set down to
weep, when to their unutterable surprise the Prince
of Glory walks out on celestial battlements and pro-
claimed His espousal of the lost cause, when they
take down their harps, tuned them to sweeter and
richer anthems and make heaven reverberate with
their dulcet melodies of redeeming grace and dying
love, down from the shining seats above, in joyful
haste He fled, enters the grave in mortal flesh and
dwelt among the dead; (oh for the love that rocks
and hills their lasting silence break, and all harmoni-
ous human tongues, the Savior's praises speak, angels assist our mighty joys, strike all your harps of
gold; but when you reach your highest notch, His
love can ne'er be told!) not all harps above can make
a heavenly place, if God His residence remove or
but conceal His face, (to thee and thee alone the
angels owe their bliss, they curl round their blaz-
ing throne and dwelt where Jesus is; infinite desire, and yet how far from thee I lie,   Oh   Jesus
raise me higher!)
    (i) Total depravity is a great fundamental Bible
truth, not meaning   as many erroneously   believe,
the ultimatum of wickedness, i.e. as bad as can be,
which does not apply even to the devil who like all
other finite beings is progressive, getting worse

all the time and will forever, as when great archangel Lucifer fell in heaven Isa. 14:12, "How art thou fallen, O Lucifer the son of the morning," he lost his hold on God in a fruitless aspiration to augment his archangelhood with a participation of the Godhead, and thus becoming a rival of our blessed Omnipotent Omniscient, Omnipresent and in falli- ble Heavenly Father; but the signification of total depravity is simply and entire deprived of the divine life which is superaboundingly revealed in both testaments by the strong monosylable "dead" Eph. 2:1 "you hath He quickened, who were dead in trespasses and in sins." Quicken is **zooeepoiceese**, from **zooee**, life; and **poieoo**, to create. Consequently you see it is a wonderfully strong word signifying to create the divine life in the dead soul. Until this is done man is an incarnate demon and doomed to the bottomless pit, which is simply God's penitentiary for the carcaration of the incorrigible subjects of His universal empire. All the unregenerated people on the earth are citizens of the devil's kingdom and nothing to do but drop out of this body into hell, which is the capital of the devil's kingdom. If we stay with him and grieve the Holy Spirit, till God sees we will not let Him save us and it would really be a mercy to take us out of the world, as the longer we live in it, the more sins we commit, and the more terrible will be our punishment in hell. Therefore mercy says cut him down, why cumbereth he the ground. Matt, 3: 10 "now the ax is laid at the root of the tree, and every tree which does not produce good fruit, is hewn down and cast into the fire. The unregenerate are all bad trees, bearing the bitter, poisonous apples of Sodom, and must be cut down if they are not, let our wonderful Omnipotent Christ, create the divine life in them; thus making them new creatures; in regeneration, the deadly upas tree having been cut down by the gospel axe, and in sanctification, all the roots taken out, by the powerful dynamite of the Holy Ghost, purifying the soul soil, but the illumination of all the obnoxious roots and even the little rootlets and spungioles of the deadly upas trees, taken out, so there will be nothing left to sprout up and produce more obnoxious pestilential trees.

CHAPTER II

HOW SHALL I GET READY TO MEET GOD?

As in the preceeding investigations you see, the utter ruin of humanity in the fall the whole head sick, the whole heart faint, not but wounds, bruises and putrifying sores," which had not been bound up and molified with ointment Isa. 1 ch. Not only full of incurable ailments, from top to toe but actually, a loathsome spiritual corpse, stenchy and pestilential. Christ says "I am the resurrection and the life" John 11 ch., in regeneration He raises dead Lazarus into life, although He had been dead those four days and putrified from top to toe. Having thus raised him so that he got up and walked out of the sepulchre, He bade them "loose him and let him go," when he became a flaming preacher of the gospel the remnant of his life, the removal of all his grave clothes and every encumbrance, brilliantly signifying our sanctification, which disencumbers us of lodgery, sectarianism, politics, all sorts of evil tempers, envy, jealousy, prejudice, bigotry, egotism, ambition, covetousness, pride, vanity, lust, passion temper and all sorts of impurities, tobacco in all its forms and phases, completely delivering us from the filthy god as nothing filthy or unclean can enter heaven, which is perfectly pure as God Himself 1 Cor. 7: 1, "Therefore let us cleanse ourselves from all the filthiness of the flesh and spirit, perfecting holiness in the fear of God; justification having made us free from sin on us condemnatory, and sanctification having made us free from sin is us contaminatory Rom. 6:22. Rest assured that without this complete and glorious emancipation and purification from sin within and without, we can never meet God nor pass the pearly portal, walk the golden streets and play on a golden harp.

(j) Therefore we must have the supernatural birth which comes down from God out of heaven, John 3: 7, "You must be born from above." If Satan can possibly utilize his preachers to sidetrack you; run you into delusions and keep you from receiving this glorious supernatural birth, by sending you down to a river to take the water god, thus running you into idolatry, he is sure to do it. You see Nicodemus though a preacher thought our Savior meant an operation performed on his body, responding to Jesus, "How can a man be born when he is old? Can he enter the second time into his mother's womb and be born," thus showing clearly that he thought Jesus meant his mortal body; when He told him positively "that born of water and spirit" had nothing to do with his body, but it was a purely spiritual transaction. Hear His response (v 6) that which is generated by depravity is depravity, that which is generated of spirit is spirit." Sarx in this passage, translated flesh, does not mean the human body at all, which is sooma, but depravity, confirmatory of the indisputable fact here enforced so emphatically on Nicodemus, not only correcting his egregious mistake, thinking that He meant an operation performed on his body, but even castigating him for his ignorance, reminding him that he was a teacher in Israel and should have known better; proceeding (v 7) to certify, "marvel not that I said unto you, you must be born from above" the English says "again' one of those unfortunate mistakes, abounding in King Jame's trans-

lation, because the Greek from which it is made had
come through the Dark Ages, a thousand years,
meanwhile not one man in a thousand nor one woman in twenty thousand could read or write; God in
His signal mercy and beneficient providence, having
all that time preserved His precious Word, unadult-
erated from the apostolic pen in the advent of St.
Katherine on Mt. Sinai, built in the second century,
to commemorate the giving of the law, on the very
spot where He had revealed it to Moses, 3,582 years
ago, and marvelously revealed it to His faithful
prophet Tichendorf of Germany, after hunting for
it forty years, A. D. 1859, the very year I graduated
from college, and sent me all the way from Germany,
the first book made from the parchment roll, which
I have read and expounded in my round, the world
ours, and translated into the beautiful Anglo-Saxon,
for the benefit of the English speaking world.

(k) The Greek **anoothen**, in this passage, never
does mean again; has but the one meaning "above,"
showing plainly that the supernatural birth comes
down from God out of heaven, and is the **sine qua non**
of every human soul, without which he will never
walk through the pearly gates and play on the gold-
en harps. Hence we do not have to go down to the
river to get it, but climb to the mountain of God,
seeking with the whole heart, testing His infallible
promise never to cast us away, but "saved to the
uttermost all that come unto God through Christ,
Heb. 7: 25. (v. 8) "The wind bloweth where it list-
eth thou heareth the sound thereof but canst not tell
whence it cometh, nor whither it goeth" should
read, "the spirit breathes on whom He will, thou
heareth His voice, but cans't not tell when He cometh, nor whither He goeth, even so is every one
who is born of the spirit. Oh how beautiful are the
words of Jesus! Every sinner is a spiritual corpse,

till the Holy Spirit breathes into him the breath of
Heavenly life. A dead man has ears, but cannot
hear, till Jesus raises him from the dead, when he
hears with his ears and sees with his eyes and leaps
with the elasticity of his newly found joy. How the
translators ever got wind into this verse is a profound mystery, as **pneuma,** beginning and ending
this verse, has no meaning but spirit.

(1) N. B. In reading your Bible you should pay no
attention to chapters and verses, as they are not in
the original, but were inserted by the translators as
a matter of their own convenience in handling the
Bible and have thereby published their ignorance to
the multiplied millions reading it in all ages and nations, as these divisions frequently break the sub-
ject in two in the middle, and consequently should
be utterly ignored by the readers. Wink at the
fourth chapter division and you will immediately run
into His sermon to the Samaritan woman at Jacob's well, in which He perpetuates the same precious
fundamental truth, involved to Nicodemus; to whom
He mentioned the water but once, whereas to the
woman seven times; impressing her indubitably that
He meant the water in Jacob's well 90 feet deep,
sparkling in its beauty for which she had come a
mile; but He corrected her mistake, telling her twice
over that He did not mean material water, but the ·
water given by Himself springing up into eternal
life. The inspired history clearly reveals that this
poor woman down at the bottom of slumdum, living
with her fifth husband, the one unwedded; pungent-
ly convicted by His straight lightning truth, inter-
penetrating her spirit and revealing all the hidden
things of darkness buried by Satan in the deep in-
terior, and developing in her life that black boycot
of sin and damnation; superinducing bottom rock
repentance and inspiring receptive faith, so she actually got the water of life and consequently like

brilliantly converted people we have so often seen
forgetting her water pot and the water, for which
she walked two miles, and running like a race horse
back to the city, preaching on the streets till she
aroused all the people, thrilled and electrified with
unutterable wonder, because the notorious repro-
bate, the stench of the city had been so wonderfully
regenerated as they also beyond the possibility of
a doubt, and consequently, in pell mell multitudes,
gladly followed her back to see the wonderful preacher, instrumental in the paradoxical change, whom
she assured them to be the Christ of prophecy, consequently they constrained Him to halt two days in
His journey, from Jerusalem to Galilee, preaching
His glorious gospel, meanwhile many got saved.

(m) Isa. 50 ch. "Ho! every one that thirsteth, come
ye to the waters and drink." Read that chapter and
you see His whole sermon is on the Christ of prophecy; here calling Him the water of life. He has
always been on the earth, excarnate in the old dis-
pensation, cognomened Jehovah and incarnate in the
new, in the blessed personage of the Jesus born in
Bethlehem, crucified and ascended to heaven and
now interceding for a lost world, coming soon to
judge the quick and the dead in righteousness, 'sit
down on the throne of David and reign over the
house of Jacob for ever, of His kingdom there shall
be no end." You see clearly from these scriptures
that Christ Himself is the water of life, of which we
must all be born, or forever lost. Eph. 2:1, "you
hath He quickened, who were dead in trespasses and
in sins; this beautiful Greek **zooee poieese**, from zoo-
ee, life, and **poieoo, t**o create, and consequently simply means He has created life in you. No one can
commit sin and retain spiritual life; as God positively says Ezek. 18: 4, 20, "the soul that sinneth it
shall die; indisputably revealing the fact that every sinner is a spiritual corpse, and so remains till

the Holy Ghost creates the divine life in Him. This
is the Christ life, i. e. the water of life, we must all
have or eternally abide in death.

(n) Therefore you see the plain, clear and un-
equivocal revelation, that the Holy Spirit must
create the divine life in every human spirit or hell
is its inevitable doom, that life is the water and the
Holy Ghost the spirit John 3:5 "Born of water and
spirit, and not a drop of material water in a million
miles. Beware of Satan's false prophets who will
tell you that it is the water that flows down the
creek, take you there and put you in it; deceived
and humbugged by the awful delusion, that you have
satisfied this scripture, "Born of water and spirit"
when like Simon Magnus Acts 8 ch. he was still in
the gall of bitterness and bond of iniquity, and sure
of hell if you do not get born of the water of life,
i. e., Christ and the Holy Ghost, who is the spirit,
who executes the glorious work of creating the divine life in the dead soul of the penitent believer.
Therefore you see you need neither a Mormon prophet nor a Campbellite preacher to put you in the water, nor a Catholic priest, nor a Protestant preacher
to sprinkle you; but "seek the Lord with all your
heart," responsively to the convictions of the Holy
Ghost and He will create in you a new heart, and put
within you a new spirit and you will pass triumphantly out of death into life with shouts of victory,
over the world, the flesh and the devil. Mark 16: 16,
"He that believeth and is baptized shall be saved" is
another passage awfully perverted and manipulated
by false prophets, for the delusion and damnation
of souls. The Bible reveals a baptism for the soul,
which Jesus gives with the Holy Ghost and fire,
Matt. 3: 11 which is also symbolized with water administered by the preacher, Ezek. 36:25, Psalm 77
ch. Isa. 52: 15, and Heb. 9: 19, etc. Now does the
above passage apply to the body or to the soul? A

school boy of a dozen years, is competent to analyze the sentence and see for himself that it does not apply to the body, which does not believe anything. Hence you see it cannot be body faith, whereas it is equally true that it is not body salvation, as the body of the Christian dies just like the sinner, and they are buried side by side in the same graveyard. Therefore no intelligent person can fail to see, that these pronouns refer directly and exclusively to the human soul, which believes on Jesus and He baptizes and saves it, and not a drop of water in a million miles; as material water cannot possibly touch the human soul. Hence these passages are murderously manipulated by Cambpellite preachers, Mormon prophets, and Catholic priests, to the humbuggery, delusion and damnation of never dying souls.

(p) Therefore if you get ready to meet God, as in the Bible times climb a Holy Mountain (made holy by the presence of God, blessing, saving and sanctifying your soul) instead of joining the church (which is right in its place, as Comeoutism is also a hell-hatched heresy for God made the church a blessed fellowship we all need) and take you to the water, instead of seeking the Lord with all your heart, soul and strength, till you find Him, let the time be long or short, taking courage from the exhortation of His prophet "Though He tarry, wait for it, as it will surely come and not tarry." The blessed Holy Ghost is invariably witnessed to His work, Rom. 8: 16. "The spirit Himself beareth witness with our spirit, that we are the children of God. A Methodist Bishop, not more than one of his members in twenty enjoyed the witness of the Holy Ghost to regeneration. Oh alarming, as that church is one of the most evangelical and spiritual in the world, and her deficiency is doubtless more fearfully verified in other communions. If you have not the clear witness of the Holy Spirit, bearing witness

with your spirit that your sins are all forgiven, and
your soul regenerated, i.e. "born from above," the
thing for you to do, is to seek the Lord with all your
heart, till you find Him, lest with Dives, that great
and benevolent church man, Luke 16 ch., you shall
lift up your eyes in hell being in torments, like him
unutterably surprised, as he died fully expecting
heaven; never having been born from above, but
depended on churchisms and his own goo works, as
you must not think that Lazarus was the only beg-
gar who subsisted on his benefactions, as Satan is
on the throne of the world, 2 Cor. 6: 4. God's un-
compromising rival, not only transforming himself,
which he well understands as he long lived in that
capacity, antecedently to his fatal apostasy, Jer.
14: 12; but even having the audacity to metamor-
phose himself and play God on the people, as we are
forced to conclude that the overwhelming majority
of normal Christians this day are so wrapped in
these diabolical delusions, as actually to worship the
devil instead of God, which lugubrious conclusion,
you will quickly reach by candid application of the
Bible straightedge to the Catholic and Protestant,
as we to our sorrow must confess, unblushingly certifying to the people, that they and all others sin
in thought, word and deed, and cannot keep it;
thus confessing judgment against themselves, that
they are not saved at all, much less sanctified; as a
genuine conviction, which we must have in order to
repent and seek the Lord, stops the sinning business,
for ever, and when you reach the first great work
of the Holy Spirit, regeneration, the problem of
sins eternal abnegation and elimination, is settled
forever, 1 John 3: 9 "Whosoever is born of God,
doth not commit sin, because His seed remaineth in
him, and he cannot sin for he is born from above;"
whereas (v. 8) certifies, " he that committeth sin is
of the devil, whose sin is from the beginning.

(q) It is an alarming fact that the Christian world with the exception of a mere sprinkle, denominated Holiness people, preach and profess a sinning religion, which is simply Satan's greased plank over which to slide them into hell; as they are so hallucinated by unsaved preachers, in the succession of the false prophets in the olden time, having been sent out by Satan, playing God on them, who studies assiduously to comfort their people in their sins, Satan's adroit manipulation, to hold them on till he can dump them into hell. Brother Godbey, you are preaching all these people to hell. You are mistaken; I preach no human soul to hell; but I preach character to hell. So sure as your Bible is true, all unregenerated people make their bed in hell. You see from the above scripture that regenerated people cannot commit sin. Therefore all this innumerable host, 450 million Catholics, 300 million Mohammedans, and 100 million Protestants, all preaching and professing a sinning religion, are not Christians, but sinners, exposed to wrath and hell. As Satan is on the throne of the world, as he is a perfect adept, playing the angel of light; his powerful intellect laid under contribution to argue down the feeble pilgrims, till they acquiesce in his vile sophistry, go to his frolics in order to win the people for the church, hold festivals, grab bags and socials to raise money for the church; thus grieving the Holy Spirit, till they backslide, lose their hold on God, die in the Church, utilized by the pastor in his funeral sermon, for their loyalty and eminent usefulness; their coffins piled with flowers, the cost of which should have been given to the missionaries in heathen fields, as well as that of the hearse and everything else that could have been economized; meanwhile they lift

up their eyes in hell, along with disappointed Dives,
Luke 16 ch.

(r) While Satan caps the climax, playing the
angel, he also claims to be God "showing himself
off that he is God," 2 Thess. 2 ch; so adroitly utilizing his powerful intellect as actually to capture the
great majority of Christendom, this day audaceous-
ly professing a sinning religion, actually led by their
own pastors, preaching and professing it, and the
people, so consummately humbugged by the devil
through their preacher, that they will not tolerate
the gospel at all, i.e. "the dynamite of God unto
salvation to every one that believeth Rom 1: 16,"
because if you believe it, a sinner, it will blow the
devil out of you, and equally true, if you believe it,
a Christian, it will blow depravity out, i.e. all evil
nature, transmitted to every human soul by Satan,
through fallen Adam, our federal head, 1 Cor. 15: 22.
"In Adam all die," i.e. every human being is generated in Adam, the first, spiritually dead, full of envy,
jealousy, prejudice, bigotry, animosity, pride, vanity,
lust, fornication, adultery, lasciviousness, unclean-
ness, hypocrisy, avarice, egotism, sorcery, witch-
craft, idolatry, sectraianism, politics, lodgery, etc.
Gal. 5 ch. which nothing but the gospel dynamite
can ever blow out. This awful Satanic hotbed of
imbred sin is really a prelude of hell in the heart,
preponderantly gravitating toward the bottomless
pit; Satan having so completely captivated the
people, that if the gospel preacher comes into the
church and preaches "the everlasting gospel with
the Holy Ghost sent down from heaven." 1 Peter 1:
12, they run him out like a dog and lock the door
against him, and if not for the civil law would actually kill him, thus augmenting the long catalogue
of 200 million martyrs, already gone on before and
shouting the victory around the effulgent throne.

(s) Rest assured, if you are gong to heaven, you

you must be free from sin, on you condemnatory,
which you receive in conversion, a full justification
in heaven, through the vicarious substitutionary a-
tonement, received and appropriated by faith alone,
exercised at the end of a radical repentance, accom-
panied by confession and restitution and instantaneously followed by the regeneration of the Holy
Spirit creating the Divine life in the heart, and thus
consummating the first great work of grace; "turn-
ing you from darkness to light, from sin and Satan
unto God, that you may receive forgiveness of sins
and inheritance among the sanctified by faith in
Christ." Acts 66 ch, The great Pauline commis-
sion, including the supernatural birth of the sinner and the full sanctification of the Christian; the
former giving you freedom from sin on you condemnatory, and the latter, conferring on you the
glorious blessing of freedom from sin in you from
sin contamnatory; thus giving you a clean heart,
Christian perfection, entire sanctification, wrought
in your immortal spirit which is yourself, filling your
body from top to toe, and actually giving you victory over the world, the flesh, the devil, clearing the
way for the ingress, who will graciously, heroically
and triumphantly hold the citadel against the com-
bined powers of earth and hell; giving you but one
job through time and eternity and that is to shout
and obey, from the simple fact that He will fight
all your battles, win all your victories, actually leaving you no job, but to shout and be true; but your
perfect victory accumulating new splendor and
grander brilliancy, through the flight of eternal
ages.

(t) Reader, are you there? "O Brother Godbey,
sad to say, no, as it is too hard for me." There is
where you let the god of this world, 2 Cor. 4:4, de-
ceive you, to your eternal ruin, as he is determined
on your damnation, and consequently telling you

that the best you can do is to be a sinning Christan, not only committing known sins in thought, word and deed, but full of imbred sin, ie. in metamorphisms infinitesimal, machinated by Satan to hold his grip on you all this time, utilizing his antiholiness preachers to bluff you off, telling you, you cannot have full salvation in this life; but if you are Protestant, telling you that you will get it in death and go to heaven, and if a Catholic you will get it in purgatory after you die and go to heaven; both utterly false, as the fiery purgatory after death is simply another name for the devil's hell, thus enabling him to sweep in the poor deluded priest-ridden Catholics by millions; whereas the Protestant hallucination is equally false and vain, because physical death is not a spiritual transaction, really having nothing to do with your immortal spirit, but simply knocking down the body, so you have to evacuate it; as your old house rots and falls down, thus leaving you houseless and homeless, to peregrinate; so when this body dies, you move right along through all eternity, just as you were in the body; if a sinner, no place for you but hell; if a Christian no place for you but heaven; as the devil only wants his own. Consequently when the Omnipotent Savior has a chance at you, and takes all sin out of you, which He invariably does; because Omnipotence cannot find a hard job; then Satan has no use for you and if you would go down to hell he wouldn't have you; but would turn you out and set the hell hounds on your track and run you off.

(u) If you are going to heaven, you must tip your hat to the devil, bidding him a long adieu and leaving him forever; at the same time giving him back all your sins, actual, original, hereditary, sins of ignorance, and infirmities and taking Jesus along for everything you need; utterly abandoned and eternally given up to God, for this world and all others;

thus reaching believing ground, where you can have nothing to do, but by simple faith take Jesus for everything and raise the shout of victory, of which the angels will never hear the last; thus reaching the altitude of His own sinless humanity, so when the devil comes to you he will find nothing in you belonging to him, and consequently cannot do anything with you; but crestfallen, retreat away and hunt somebody who will receive his bait and give him a chance to drag them in hell.

(v) I beg you no longer listen to Satan's lies, dispensed through his deluded votaries in pulpit and pew; as well as administered to your own heart by Satan in person, and especially his countless myrmydons which throng the air, all lying on Jesus telling you He can't give you an uttermost salvation in this life; at the same time hallucinating you with the vain hope, if a Protestant you will get it in death and if a Catholic, you will get it in purgatory; meanwhile Jesus is standing by and ready to give it to you, and the Holy Spirit grieved night and day, because you will not let Him give the help you need, for a sky blue conversion and a sunburst sanctification, giving you the shine, the shout, and the jump, the glorious victory in your soul and life which will brighten through the flight of eternal ages.

CHAPTER III

WHEN SHALL I GET READY?

This is the momentous question, roaring and reverberating in lugubrious wails; echoing repeatedly from the walls of hell and the dismal dome; eternally resounding the lugubrious wails of the damned, all of whom wrecked their barks of heavenly hope on this momentous advert, when shall I get ready to meet my God? There is not a soul among all the countless millions now weeping, wailing and gnashing their teeth in the dismal dungeons of irretrievable woe, who ever entertained the remotest idea of culminating in this terrific and irretrievable wreckage; but everyone contemplated enchanting visions in charming panaroma moving before them, amid which in their electrified anticipations they heard angels shouting, seraphim singing and golden harps ringing, and now eternally lift up their mournful confessions, "When young life's journey began, the glittering prospect charmed my eyes; I saw a long the extended plain, joy after joy successive rise; But soon I found 'twas all a dream, And should have learned the fond pursuit to shun, Here few can reach their purposed end, And thousands daily are undone!

(w) Satan's hackneyed maxim, he constantly rings in the ears of his deluded voraries, "time enough yet" I heard it reverberate from the lips of an octogenarian infidel in old Yankee land, tottering on the verge of his grave and still saying that he would live for this world alone while in it and let every world take care of itself; whereas this world is simply the preparatory for eternity, rushing on us at locomotive speed. Really there is no time for us, but the present fleeting moment as God constantly rings in our ears, now is the accepted time, now is the day of salvation! If you hear His voice harden not your heart, i.e. do not reject it. On arrival in this room I received a letter from my elect sister J. H. Geatrix, of Vancouver, B. C. Canada, stating that her noble preaching husband by whose side I have often stood on the battle field, dropped dead in the pulpit, preaching in the salvation army hall. Bob Ingersoll, the great infidel, arose in the morning to all appearances in perfect health, sat down at the table, ate his breakfast, looked over the papers for newsy items and died instantaneously; after years of earnest and importunate warnings; on one occasion a S. A. officer having personally preached to him two solid hours in the car. How exceedingly common now days for people to drop dead instantaneously! I have just returned from my native land Southern Ky. where I preached ten years in five churches and tabernacles to crowded audiences; having felt a great anxiety to meet two of my neighborhood boys, schoolmates the first 20 years of my life and still surviving; but they both dropped dead in their tracks only a few days before my arrival; members of the Campbellite church in which they neither preach the supernatural birth for the sinner nor entire sanctification for the Christian, both of which the Bible positively certifies sina qua nons. As they are really infidels appertaining to the Holy Ghost and idolaters on immersion, recognizing it essential to salvation, whereas it is not found in the Bible, Old nor New, nor anything else which has that meaning, a native latin word and would abound in the Latin Bible which was made in the Apostolic Age, if it had been the practice of John the Baptist and the Apostles, but it does not occur anywhere from lid to lid; thus with sundry corroberative inspired testimonies, irrefutably, uning the incontestable fact it was utterly unknown know in the apostolic age Lactantious the oldest historian in the Christian era certifying "John the Baptist sprinkled Peter and Peter sprinkled and Christ sent His own Apostles to sprinkle the nations; whereas Mark 1:8, Luke 3: 16, Act 1: 5 and 11: 16, Heb. 10: 22, involving the testimony of John the Baptist, Jesus, Peter, Paul, Mark, Luke and Apollos all certifying that they handled the water and not the people; the stature of Jesus and Paul, representing them standing and John the Baptist and Ananias, pouring the water on their heads as I have repeatedly seen with my own eyes.

(x) As these men were the comrades of my childhood and youth, I was anxious to meet them again before they went out of life, look them in thte face and tell them the blessed truth by which we are saved, sanctified, and prepared to meet God. I preach no soul to hell, as I know not what God may do for them before they pass out of life; but we must preach character to hell, as God in His Word so clearly explicitly and unequivocally certifies over and over, "line upon line and precept upon precept," that we must be born from above John 3: 7 and sanctified wholly Heb. 12: 14, 1 Thess. 5: 23 if we ever pass through the pearly gates and abide in the presence of an infinitely holy God, among unfallen angels, who have never known sin nor sorrow and the innumerable host of redeemed spirits "Who have washed their robes and made them white in the blood of the lamb, having come up through great tribulations, as Satan contests irresistably every inch of our journey from the city of destruction to the celestial metropolis.

(y) When we contemplate the awful danger of grieving away the Holy Spirit by whose conviction, regeneration, sanctification, and glorification alone is our salvation possible. Every human soul longs for heaven and dreads hell, and really expects to escape the latter and gain the former, but

wait too long. As an incontestable demonstration of
its utter fallacy, the voter in of infidelity, all gave
it up, before they land in hell; if not on or before
their deathbed, they realize its utter falsity, when
they see hell opened and coming to meet them and
the demons already on hand with their flanking
chains which has been the testimony of so many
dying reprobates. Tom Payne, the champion Apostle
of infidelity, when he came to die had all the infidels excluded from the room and spent his last
hours pleading with Jesus to save his soul; thus re-
nouncing his lifelong ministry, preaching Satan's
gospel for the damnation of the world, which he
so successfully manipulated to populate hell through
the rolling centuries. Such is the testimony of his
nurse in the providence of God, a noble quakeress,
who witnessed his expiring agonies, pleading with
the Jesus, he had denounced, to save his soul.

Apostolic Holiness Sunday School Literature

APOSTOLIC BIBLE TEACHER
A Monthly Journal for Sunday School
Teachers

THE ADVANCED QUARTERLY
Prepared for the Advanced Sunday School
Classes

YOUNG PEOPLE'S QUARTERLY
For Intermediate Sunday School Classes

THE CHILDREN'S PAPER
Especially prepared for Primary Classes
Ably edited from a full salvation stand-
point. Will raise the spiritual life
of any Sunday School

SECRETARY'S COMPLETE RECORD
For the Secretary a whole year

TEACHER'S CLASS BOOK
For the Teacher a whole year

Samples sent free on application

Published by the

APOSTOLIC MESSENGER OFFICE

GREENSBORO, N. C.

Apostolic Messenger Office

Book and Job Printing

Reasonable Prices
High Grade Work

Quotations Gladly Submitted

---

900 Silver Run Ave., Greensboro, N. C.

www.ingramcontent.com/pod-product-compliance
Lightning Source LLC
Chambersburg PA
CBHW030313030426
42337CB00012B/690